W9-BZA-458

The Children's Book of Home and Family

EDITED BY
William J. Bennett

ILLUSTRATED BY
Michael Hague

A DOUBLEDAY BOOK FOR YOUNG READERS

The Children's Book of Home and Family

A Doubleday Book for Young Readers
Published by
Random House Children's Books
a division of Random House, Inc.
1540 Broadway
New York, New York 10036

Cataloging-in-Publication Data is available from the Library of Congress.
ISBN 0-385-74624-5 (trade)
0-385-90848-2 (lib. bdg.)
The text of this book is set in 13-point Dutch Aster.
Manufactured in the United States of America
October 2002
10 9 8 7 6 5 4 3 2 1
BVG

Contents

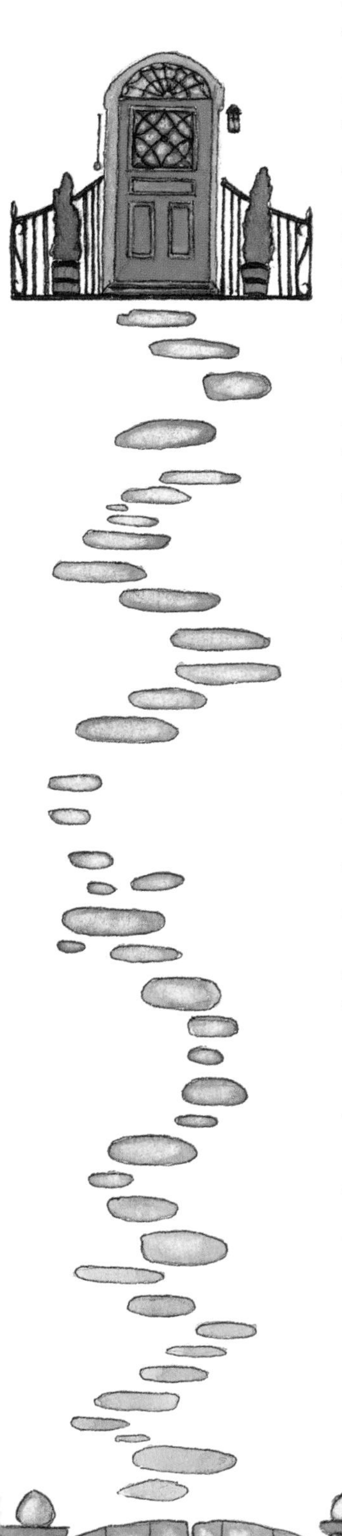

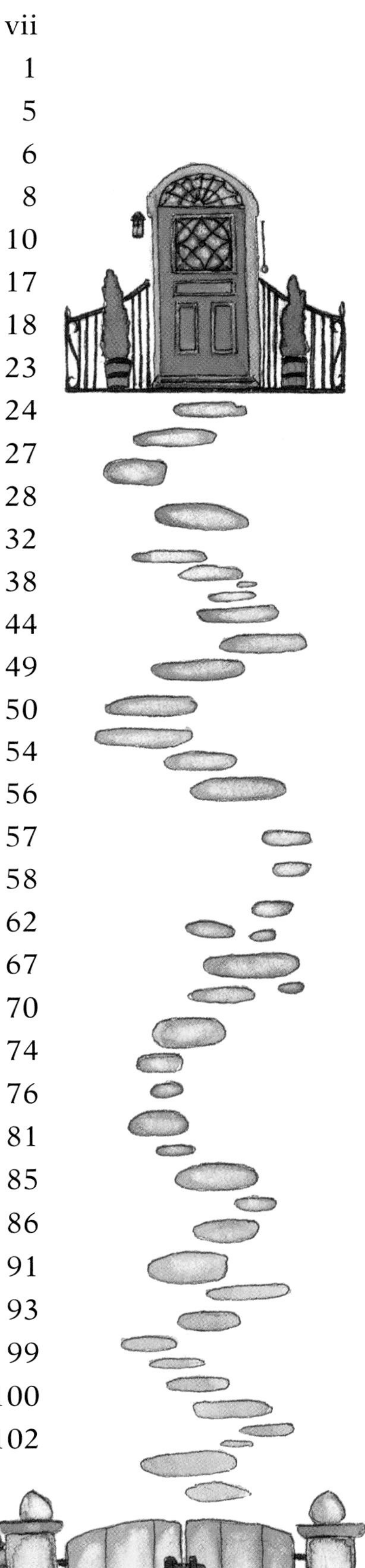

Introduction

All children need a roof to keep out the rain, walls to shelter them from the wind, a hearth to drive away the cold. Those are the basics, but they are not enough. Children also need love, order, laughter, and at least one adult who would do just about anything for them. And because children are not born knowing the difference between right and wrong, they need a place where they can begin to develop a moral sense. They need people to guide them toward what is right and good. Home is that place. Families are those people.

"It is the peculiarity of man, in comparison with the rest of the animal world," Aristotle wrote long ago, "that he alone possesses a perception of good and evil, of the just and the unjust, and of other similar qualities; and it is association in these things which makes a family." As Aristotle knew, the qualities we call virtues are no small part of what family is all about. Transmission of those virtues is a job no other institution can fully replace. Character takes shape when children are very young, formed by the *do*s and *don't*s offered at home. It emerges under the influence of examples set by mother, father, sisters, and brothers.

The stories families share can be important moral influences too—and that is the reason for this book. All these selections center around home or family life. They provide a good way for adults and children to talk about beliefs they hold dear. They are good tools for reinforcing the vital lessons all parents must teach. Today many parents say it has gotten harder to teach those lessons. Mothers and fathers find themselves competing with opposing messages from popular culture. This book is an ally that can help adults teach fundamental virtues and help children realize the importance of family.

In these pages we find family members helping each other along and looking to each other for help. We find siblings demonstrating what brotherhood and sisterhood really mean. We see children learning about chores, responsibilities, and self-sacrifice, and learning to help their parents out of love. We witness mothers and fathers devoting time and attention to the most important task they have in life: raising their young. We see what virtues such as loyalty, courage, and perseverance mean to families, and how love of family can overcome any number of obstacles.

Such lessons stay with us long after we leave our first homes. In our affections and memories, they remain a part of us. They become moral compass points, guiding and instructing us on the rest of life's journey.

In one sense, the moral journey that begins with leaving home is the search for opportunities to offer others the same nurturing love we received in our own childhood. The best memories of home become ideals we seek to re-create in our lives and in the lives of the children we bring into the world. We start our own families, offer our own lessons, nurture our own children in the strength and knowledge we gained beside the first warm hearth of home.

Of course, no family is perfect. Home can be the place where we get our first look at vices as well as virtues. Most of us live between the perfect and the imperfect. But even though many homes fall short of the ones we find in these pages, these stories give us something to aspire to. They remind us of the conditions families need and the attentions our loved ones deserve. These examples help us raise our sights and our efforts.

Once again, Michael Hague has brought the stories I've chosen to life with his beautiful illustrations. This is our fifth collaboration. Each time, it has been a joy and a wonder to watch Michael's sketches turn into drawings and his drawings turn into works of art. I do not know how he does it, but I know that children and adults all over the world adore the results. Michael's illustrations glow with mystery and goodness and love.

I hope this book helps you pass on some important lessons to young ones you love. I hope reading these stories becomes part of your family's time together.

The Golden Windows

Who has the best house in the world? This story helps us find out.

Roberto lived on a farm way out in the country at the edge of a wide, green valley with wooded mountains all around. His house stood on top of a hill. It was a good place to live, with lots of room for a boy to roam. In the afternoons, after he finished his homework, he would feed his calf or throw sticks in the pond or just wander around the farm.

Roberto's favorite time of day was evening, just when the sun was getting ready to set. He liked to sit on his porch and look across the valley at another hill that rose in the distance. On that far hill stood an old house with windows of gold. The only time of day when he could see the windows was right before the sun went down, and then they were so bright that Roberto had to squint when he looked at them. They gleamed across the whole valley, and the boy thought it must be the most wonderful home in the world.

One Saturday Roberto decided to go see the house with windows of gold. He made a lunch and put it in his backpack. Then he said goodbye to his mother and father, promised to be careful, and started across the valley.

It was a beautiful day for a hike. The sun smiled and white clouds floated above the distant mountaintops. Roberto passed fields of wheat and pastures where cows stared at him over fences. Every once in a while a car passed him on the road. It was usually someone he knew, and he waved. His shadow walked beside him and gave him company. It was all very cheerful.

After a while he felt hungry, so he sat down beside a clear stream that ran down the middle of the valley. He ate his sandwich, an apple, and a candy bar. Then he started off again.

Finally he came to a high green hill. He trudged up the side, and there was the house on top. But when he got close, his mouth dropped open in surprise. It was just an old house like any other house, with ordinary windows made out of glass. There wasn't anything golden about them.

A woman came to the door, smiled at Roberto, and said hello.

"I saw the windows of gold from our hilltop," he said, "and I came all this way to see them up close."

The woman shook her head and laughed.

"No, I'm afraid we don't have windows of gold," she said.

"We just have glass windows, but glass is better to see through."

She invited Roberto to sit on the porch. She brought him a piece of cake and a glass of milk, and they talked for a while. Then she called her daughter, who was about Roberto's age, and went back inside the house.

The girl's name was Nancy. She led Roberto all around the farm and showed him her black calf, which had a white star on its forehead. He told her about his own calf at home, which was brown like an acorn, with four white feet.

When they had eaten an apple together and become good friends, Roberto asked her about the golden windows.

"You've come the wrong way!" Nancy said. "Come with me. I'll show you the house with the golden windows."

They walked toward a rise behind her house. As they went, Nancy told Roberto that the golden windows could be seen only at a certain hour, before sunset.

"Yes, I know that!" said Roberto.

When they reached the rise, the girl turned and pointed across the wide valley. There on a hill far away stood a house with windows of gleaming gold, just as he had seen them. When he looked again, Roberto saw that it was his own home.

He told Nancy he must go. He gave her his best pebble, the white one with the red band, which he had carried for a year in his pocket. She gave him a whistle she had gotten out of a cereal box. He promised to come again, but he did not tell her what he had learned. He hurried back down the hill, and Nancy stood in the light of the sunset and watched him.

It was almost dark when Roberto reached his own house. His family was getting ready for supper. When he opened the door, his mother came to kiss him, and his little sister ran to throw her arms around his neck. His father, who was setting the table, smiled.

"Did you have a good day?" asked his mother.

Yes, he had had a very good day.

"And did you learn anything?" asked his father.

"Yes!" said Roberto. "I learned that our house has windows of gold!"

Bless This House

This old blessing is a nice way to invite God into our homes.

Bless this house, O Lord, we pray.
Make it safe by night and day.
Bless these walls so firm and stout,
Keeping want and trouble out.

Bless the roof and chimney tall,
Let Thy peace be over all.
Bless these doors that they may prove
Ever open to joy and love.

Bless these windows shining bright,
Letting in God's heavenly light.
Bless the hearth a-blazing there
With smoke ascending like a prayer.

Bless the people here within,
Keep them pure and free from sin.
Bless us all that we may be
Fit, O Lord, to dwell with Thee.
Amen.

What Bradley Owed

—ADAPTED FROM HUGH T. KERR

Home is the place where we do many things just for love.

There was once a boy named Bradley. When he was about eight years old, he got into the habit of thinking about everything in terms of money.

"How much is your computer worth?" he asked his father.

"How much did your skates cost?" he asked his older brother.

"How much did your parents pay for their car?" he asked his friend Melissa.

He wanted to know the price of everything he saw, and if it didn't cost a lot, he didn't have a very high opinion of it.

But there are some things money can't buy. And some of them are the best things in the world.

One Saturday morning when Bradley came to the kitchen for breakfast, he put a little piece of paper, neatly folded, on his mother's plate. His mother opened it, and she could hardly believe it, but this is what her son had written:

Mom owes Bradley:	
For running errands	$3
For taking out the trash	$2
For sweeping the floor	$2
Extras	$1
Total that Mom owes Bradley	$8

His mother smiled when she read that, but she did not say anything.

When lunchtime came, she put the bill on Bradley's plate along with eight dollars. Bradley's eyes lit up when he saw the money. He stuffed it into his pocket as fast as he could and started dreaming about what he would buy.

Then he saw that there was another piece of paper beside his plate, neatly folded, just like the first one. When he opened it, he found it was a bill from his mother. It read:

Bradley owes Mom:	
For being good to him	$0
For nursing him through his chicken pox	$0
For his shirts and shoes and toys	$0
For his meals and beautiful room	$0
Total that Bradley owes Mom	$0

Bradley sat looking at this new bill, not saying a word. After a few minutes he got up, pulled the eight dollars out of his pocket, and placed them in his mother's hand.

And after that, he helped his mother for love.

Mr. Nobody

Does this fellow live at your house?

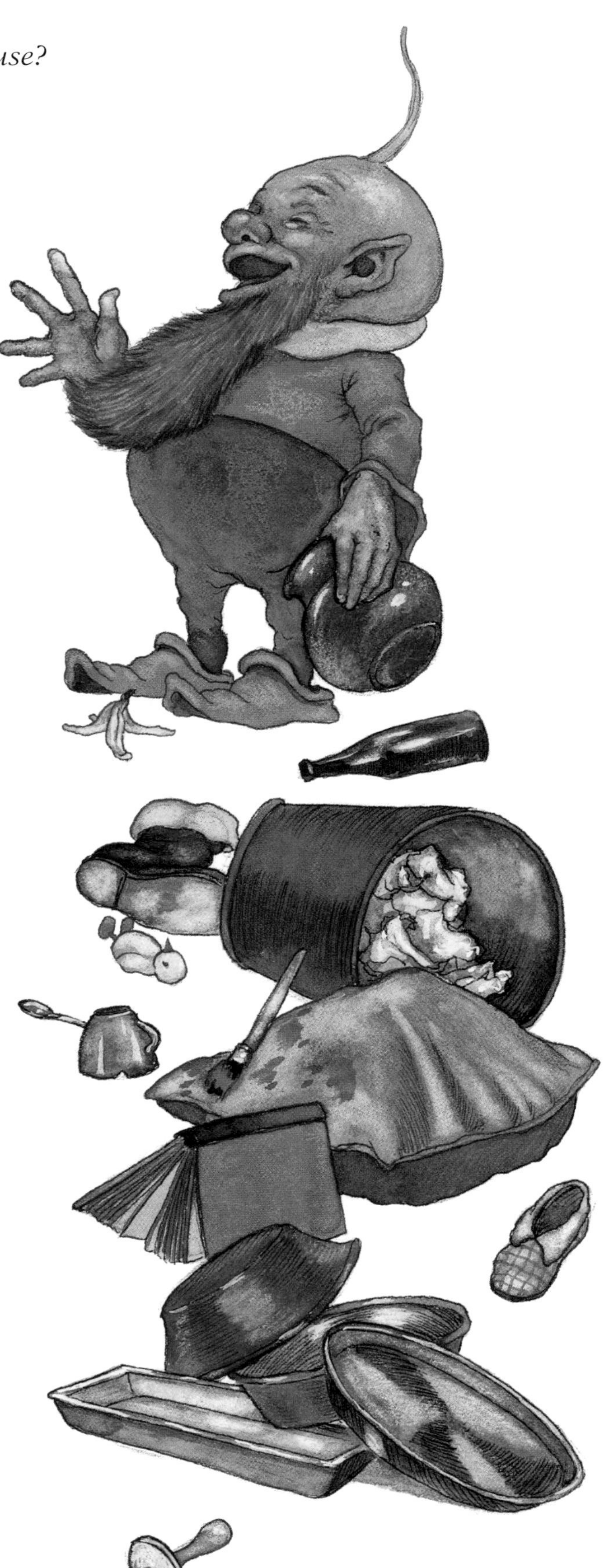

I know a funny little man
As quiet as a mouse,
Who does the mischief that is done
In everybody's house!
No one ever sees his face,
And yet we all agree
That every plate we break was cracked
By Mr. Nobody.

It's he who always tears our books,
Who leaves the door ajar;
He pulls the buttons from our shirts
And scatters clothes afar.
That squeaking door will always squeak,
For, really, don't you see,
We leave the oiling to be done
By Mr. Nobody.

He leaves the lights on everywhere
And never picks up toys.
He hopes the cleaning will be done
By other girls and boys.
The papers always are mislaid—
Who had them last but he?
There's no one tosses them about
But Mr. Nobody.

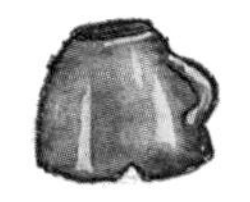

The finger marks upon the door
  Are never left by us.
We never leave our bikes outside
  Where they can sit and rust.
Our juice we never spill, the boots
  That lying round you see
Are not our boots. They all belong
  To Mr. Nobody.

The Water of Youth

—Adapted from Rudolph Baumbach

Marriage gives husbands and wives the chance to love each other more and more with each passing year.

It was Midsummer Day. The heat of noon brooded over the cornfields, and the air was full of chirping grass-hoppers.

Along a path in the forest came a slim young bride in a peasant dress, with a basket on her arm and a jug in her hand. Greta was her name, and she was on her way to see her husband, Hans, who was cutting wood.

"Stand back!" Hans shouted when he saw her. "The tree is falling!" A great fir tree groaned, bent its head, and came crashing down.

Then Greta walked on, and the brown-faced woodcutter took his young wife in his arms and kissed her tenderly. They sat down and unpacked the basket of food Greta had brought. Just as they started to eat, Hans jumped up, grabbed his ax, and cut three marks on the stump of the tree he had cut down.

"What is that for?" asked his wife.

"For the little old women of the woods," he said. "Their enemy, the wild huntsman, lies in wait for them day and night and sets his dogs on them. But if the poor little things can reach a tree stump marked like that, the wild huntsman cannot touch them."

Greta opened her eyes wide. "Have you ever seen one of the little folk?"

"No, they seldom show themselves. But this is Midsummer Day, so perhaps we might see one." He called into the forest: "Little woman of the woods, come out!" He only meant to tease his wife, but on Midsummer Day it is not safe to make jokes like that.

All of a sudden there stood before them a lovely little old lady in a quaint little dress, with a bonnet on her head. The young people jumped up in astonishment.

"You called at just the right moment," said the little old woman. She pointed at the stump with the three marks. "One good turn deserves another. Follow me."

Hans thought he knew every inch of the forest, but he had never seen the spot to which the little old woman of the woods led them. They came upon a tiny house not much higher than your knee. The roof was made with the scales of

pinecones, every scale pinned down with a rose thorn. Behind the house was a spring with irises and lilies growing on the brink. Gold-and-green dragonflies danced over its water.

"This is the spring of youth," said the little woman. "If you drink the water, it will keep you young and strong until your dying day. Fill your jug and carry it home. One drop every Sunday will be enough to keep you young." Then she vanished into her house.

Hans and Greta filled the jug and hurried home to their cottage. Hans poured the water into a bottle, sealed it with fir resin, and put it in a cupboard.

"Just now we have no use for the water of youth," he said. "We can save it up till we do need it."

A year went by, full of love and happiness. And then there was a rosy baby boy, who kicked and gurgled till his father's heart overflowed with pride.

"Now is the time to open our bottle," said Hans. "Don't you think a drop would do you good, Greta?"

He went to fetch it from the next room. His hands trembled so with his joy, though, that the bottle slipped from his grasp and shattered on the floor. Hans was horrified. He did not want to disappoint Greta, so he got another bottle, filled it with ordinary springwater, and brought it to his wife.

"Ah!" said Greta. "How that gives me new life and strength! Take a drop yourself, my dear."

Hans obeyed her and said what a wonderful drink it was. After that they each took a drop every Sunday when the bells called them to church. Hans tried to find the spring of youth in the woods again, but though he looked and looked, he could never find the spot.

Two more years went by. A second baby was born, a rosy girl who came to keep her brother company. Greta's round chin grew double, but she never noticed it, for there were no mirrors in those days. Hans noticed it but said nothing and loved his wife more than ever.

Then one day when Greta was not looking, her little boy got into the cupboard where the bottle was kept, knocked it over, and broke it.

"Oh, no!" cried Greta. "What will I do?" With trembling fingers, she picked up the pieces of glass. She did not want to disappoint Hans, so she got another bottle, filled it with springwater, and put it in the cupboard.

Time passed. Hans and Greta each took care not to let the other think their youth was gone, and every Sunday they took the magic drop.

One day Hans found a gray hair in his comb and decided he should tell his wife that he had spilled all the water of youth. Heavy of heart, he began, "Look! I'm getting old."

Greta was startled but quickly recovered. "Why, that's nothing. I had a gray hair when I was ten. You're just as young as ever! No, dear Hans, the magic water keeps us young, or"—she glanced at him nervously—"do you think I am growing old too?"

Hans laughed. "You—old? You're as fresh as a daisy." He threw his arms around her portly figure and kissed her.

When he was alone he said joyfully, "She has no idea that we are growing old. So what I did must have been the right thing." And his wife said just the same thing to herself.

Many years passed. The children grew up and left home. They married and had children of their own. The two old people were alone together once more. They were just as much in love with each other as on their wedding day, and every Sunday, while the church bells were ringing, they each took one drop out of the bottle.

In the evenings, when the young lads and lasses of the village danced to the music of a strolling fiddler, no couple jigged and hopped under the trees more merrily than Hans and Greta. Wherever they went, they held hands like young sweethearts. Sometimes they sat together in front of their house and sang little songs about true love. People passing by said, "What silly old folk!" But the happy pair did not hear them.

One Midsummer Day the old couple walked into the forest for a picnic. After a while, they came to an old fir tree and spread a little feast out of Greta's basket.

"It was right here," said Hans, "that the little old woman of the forest appeared to us that day. I would like to see her again and thank her for the gift she gave us. Let's go look for her. Maybe we'll be as lucky as we were before."

They rose and went into the heart of the forest. They had walked only a little way when suddenly the spot with the tiny house stood before them.

With fast-beating hearts they walked around the house, and there was the spring of youth with the gold-and-green dragonflies hovering over it. Hand in hand, they bent over the water. Out of its clear depths two gray heads with kindly, wrinkled faces gazed back at them.

Hot tears rushed to their eyes, and with sobs they told each other what they had done. It was some time before they understood that for all those years they both had been hiding what had happened for love's sake.

"So you knew we were both growing old?" asked Hans.

"Of course I did!" his wife laughed through her tears.

"So did I!" cried Hans. He took his wife's face in his hands and kissed her, just as he had on the day they were married.

Suddenly, as if she had sprung out of the earth, the little old woman of the woods stood before the old couple.

"Welcome!" she said. "It has been long since you came to visit me. But what is this? You have not taken care of the water of youth. Wrinkles and gray hairs! This will never do. You've come just at the right moment. Quick! Jump into the spring—it is not deep. All the strength and beauty of youth will come back to you. You can have whole new lives!"

Hans and Greta looked at each other.

"Will you?" he asked in a voice that shook.

"Never!" answered Greta promptly. "I can't tell you what bliss it is that at last I can be old. Just think of all the good times we will have with our grandchildren. I would not give those up! No, dear little woman, we thank you with all our hearts, but we will stay old. Won't we, Hans?"

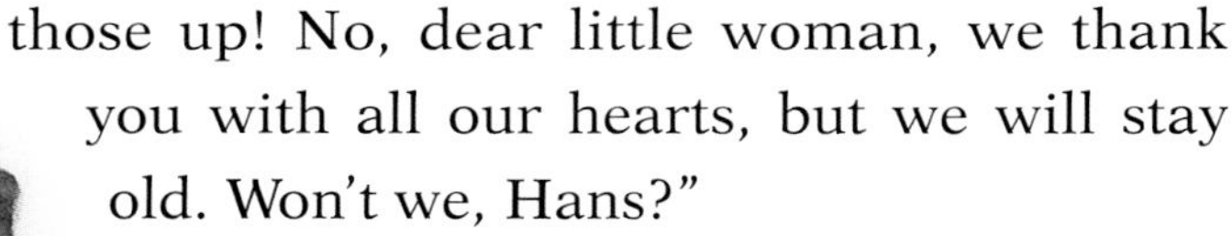

"Yes!" said Hans. "We will stay old. Hooray! Greta, if you only knew how well your gray hair suits you!"

"Well, if you wish," said the little woman. "I won't insist." And with a rather offended air she went into her house and shut the door.

The old folk kissed each other once more and turned toward home. Arm in arm, they went through the forest, and the midsummer sun set a crown of gold on their gray heads.

The Robin to His Mate

This little poem teaches a lot about what husbands and wives do.
They love each other, work together, and build a home for their family.

Said Robin to his pretty mate,
  "Bring here a little hay.
Lay here a stick and there a straw,
  And bring a little clay.

"And we will build a little nest,
  Where you quite soon will lay
Your little eggs, so smooth, so blue.
  Come, let us work away.

"And you will keep them very warm,
  And only think, my dear,
It won't be long before we see
  Four little robins here!"

Ruth and Naomi

Here is one of the world's great stories about loyalty and love of family. It comes from the Book of Ruth in the Bible.

A long while ago, hard times came to the land of Israel. The crops in the fields dried up and turned brown. The cattle and sheep grew sick and thin. Before long, people were running out of food.

In the town of Bethlehem, a woman named Naomi lived with her husband, Elimelech, and two sons. Like all the Israelites, Naomi's little family was struggling. Every day their supply of food grew smaller and smaller. They looked at each other with sadness in their eyes, because they knew it wouldn't be long before they had nothing left to eat.

So Naomi and Elimelech made a very hard decision. They decided to leave their homeland and move to a country called Moab. They did not want to go any more than you would want to pick up and move far away to a strange place where you did not have a single friend. But they knew it was best for their family to go, so they set their faces to the east and left Bethlehem in search of food.

After several days of traveling, they came to the land of Moab. When they saw the fields fat with grain and orchards thick with fruit, they knew they had done the right thing, and soon they were settled in their new home.

Naomi's sons both found wives in Moab. One of these young women was named Ruth. She was a beautiful girl with a warm smile and a gentle spirit. Ruth and Naomi would laugh and tell stories while they baked bread or drew water from the well. They became good friends and spent many happy years together.

Then tragedy struck. Naomi's husband, Elimelech, and both of her sons died. Suddenly Naomi felt very old and tired, and very alone in a foreign land. She knew, deep in her heart, that it was time to go back to her home.

"There is nothing to keep me here," she told Ruth. "I hear that the famine is over in Israel, so I'm going back to Bethlehem. Your place is not with me, an old, penniless woman. You must go back to your parents' house. You are young and pretty, and someday you'll marry again."

But Ruth did not want to leave Naomi. Naomi was her husband's mother. Ruth loved Naomi dearly and wanted to take care of her for the rest of her days. She threw her arms around Naomi's neck.

"Wherever you go, I will follow," she said. "Your home will be my home, your people will be my people, and your God will be my God. Where you die I will die, and there I will be buried."

When Naomi saw how much Ruth loved her, she did not argue with her anymore. The two women set out for Israel. They did not know how they would live, for they had no money. They only knew they had each other for support.

They reached Bethlehem just as the barley harvest was beginning. Now, in those days, there was a law to help poor people get food. The law said that after the farmers went through their fields cutting the grain, the poor people could follow and pick up any stalks that had been left behind. This was called gleaning.

"I will go out and glean for our food," Ruth told Naomi.

It was backbreaking work. All day long, Ruth stooped in the hot sun among the stubble, hunting for fallen grains she could pick up. She never rested or complained, though. Every day she worked to fill up her little sack, knowing that otherwise Naomi would go hungry. Naomi's old friends nodded and said how lucky she was to have Ruth looking after her.

One evening the owner of the field, a man named Boaz, noticed how hard Ruth was working. He asked his reapers who she was.

"A foreigner," one told him. "She's the girl who came from Moab to look after old Naomi."

Boaz's heart was touched. He went over to Ruth.

"You are welcome here," he said kindly. "Do not glean in anyone else's field. Take what you need, and when you get thirsty, drink the water my workers have drawn from the well."

Ruth bowed to Boaz and thanked him for his kindness.

"Why are you being so good to me?" she asked. "I am a stranger here."

Boaz smiled. "I've heard about how you left your home to take care of Naomi," he said. "May God reward you for what you've done. You will always be safe here."

When lunchtime came, Boaz brought some bread for Ruth. "Dip your bread in this wine," he told her. She sat with the reapers and ate until she was full.

When lunch was over, Boaz spoke to his reapers.

"Take good care of this young woman," he told them. "Make sure she gets all the grain she needs. She's had a hard life, and it's up to us to help her now."

So Ruth gleaned in the fields of Boaz as long as the harvest lasted. Every day Boaz watched her cheerfully picking up grain. Every night he watched her leave the fields and go back to Naomi, carrying grain for their bread.

The more Boaz saw the beautiful young woman from Moab, the more he liked her. There was something in her good-natured smile and quiet ways that made him want to take care of her. After a while Boaz realized that he loved this gentle girl, and that she loved him back.

Ruth and Boaz were married, and they found joy together for many years. Naomi came to live in their home and was as happy as she could be. Before long, Ruth had a baby son named Obed, and Naomi was the proudest grandmother in Bethlehem.

When Obed grew up, he had a son named Jesse. And when Jesse grew up, he had a son named David—the very same David who killed the giant Goliath with his slingshot and became the king of Israel.

And so Ruth—the kind Moabite girl who refused to leave Naomi's side—became the mother of kings.

Prayer for Home and Family

—Robert Louis Stevenson

This beautiful prayer sums up, in many ways, what family life should be.

Lord, behold our family assembled here. We thank Thee for this place in which we dwell; for the love that unites us; for the peace accorded us this day; for the hope with which we expect the morrow; for the health, the work, the food, and the bright skies that make our lives delightful; for our friends in all parts of the earth.

Let peace abound in our small company. Purge out of every heart the lurking grudge. Give us grace and strength to forbear and to persevere. Offenders ourselves, give us the grace to accept and to forgive offenders. Forgetful ourselves, help us to bear cheerfully the forgetfulness of others.

Give us courage and gaiety and the quiet mind. Spare to us our friends, soften to us our enemies. Bless us, if it may be, in all our innocent endeavors. If it may not, give us the strength to encounter that which is to come, that we may be brave in peril, constant in tribulation, temperate in wrath and in all changes of fortune, and down to the gates of death, loyal and loving one to another.

As the clay to the potter, as the windmill to the wind, as children of their sire, we beseech of Thee this help and mercy for Christ's sake.

Amen.

Cornelia's Jewels

In this world, there are many ways to be rich.
Here is one way that really matters.

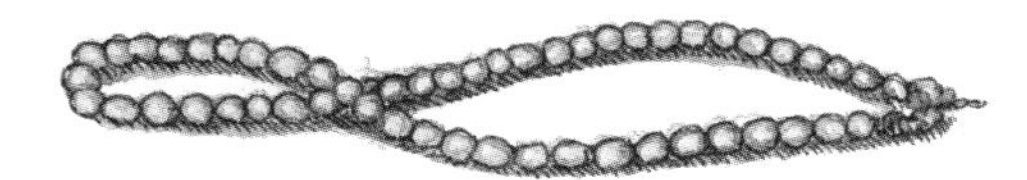

It was a bright summer morning in the old city of Rome. Two brothers were playing in a garden when their mother, Cornelia, called them.

"An old friend of mine is coming to see us today," she said. "She is very rich, and she will probably show us her jewels."

Soon the woman arrived. Her fingers sparkled with rings. Her arms glittered with bracelets. Chains of gold hung around her neck, and strands of pearls gleamed in her hair.

"Did you ever see anyone so pretty?" the older boy whispered to his brother. "She looks like a queen!"

They gazed at their own mother, who had no glittering stones. She wore a simple white robe. Her hands and arms were bare, and for a crown she had only the soft brown hair that curled about her head. But her kind smile seemed to light her face more than any bright gem could.

"Would you like to see more of my treasures?" the rich woman asked. She called to one of her servants, who brought a box and set it on a table. When the lady opened it, there were heaps of red rubies, sapphires as blue as the summer sky, emeralds as green as the sea, and diamonds that flashed like sunlight.

The boys looked at the gems for a long time. Then they looked at each other. "I wish our mother could have beautiful things like these," the younger one whispered to his brother.

After a while the box was closed and carried away.

"Tell me, Cornelia," the rich woman said with a smile full of pity, "is it true you have no jewels? Are the rumors I heard true—that you are really quite poor?"

Cornelia smiled. "Not at all," she said. "I have jewels far more valuable than yours."

"Then let me see them," the rich lady laughed. "Where are they?"

Cornelia drew her two boys to her side.

"These are my jewels," she said. "Wouldn't you agree that they are far more precious than all of your gems?"

The two boys, who were named Tiberius and Caius Gracchus, never forgot their mother's love and pride. When they grew up, they became great leaders in Rome and were held in high esteem by the people. As long as they lived, they liked to think back on the scene in the garden. They never forgot their dear mother, who had shown them how to be wise and good, and who had treasured them more than all the precious stones in the world.

The Boy We Want

Here is a good code for sons to live up to.

A boy who is truthful and honest
 And faithful and willing to work;
But we have not a place that we care to disgrace
 With a boy who is ready to shirk.

Wanted—a boy you can tie to,
 A boy who is trusty and true,
A boy who is good to old people,
 And kind to the little ones too.

A boy who is nice to the home folks,
 And pleasant to sister and brother,
A boy who will try when things go awry
 To be helpful to father and mother.

These are the boys we depend on—
 Our hope for the future, and then
Grave problems of state and the world's work await
 Such boys when they grow to be men.

Monica and Augustine

Here is the story of a man who was saved by the love of his mother.

It was late at night—long past the time when boys and girls should be in bed—and a boy named Augustine was climbing into the branches of a neighbor's pear tree.

"Look out below," he whispered, and he started tearing the fruit off the limbs and tossing it to his friends on the ground. He took every pear he could find. Then he jumped down and ran off with his friends, laughing.

"These pears are no good," one of the boys said with a frown. "They're not ripe enough to eat."

"I know," said Augustine.

"Then why did we steal them?"

"Why not?" Augustine said, shrugging. "We had a good time, didn't we?"

"Sure. But what are we going to do with all this fruit?"

"Let's throw it to the pigs."

Laughing at how clever they were, the gang slouched toward the pigsty.

That's the kind of boy Augustine was. He stole from neighbors, and he stole from his parents. He lied to his friends and cheated when he played games. He was often lazy at school. When he got older, he was always sneaking off to see gladiator fights and chariot races. He grew up thinking mostly about how to get whatever he wanted and get it right away.

You would think a boy like that would come to no good. But Augustine had one wonderful thing going for him. He had a mother named Monica who loved him more than anything in the world.

Monica was a good woman, and she knew that deep down her son had much good in him too. She saw that if he would only open his heart to God, he could do great things.

Monica wept for Augustine. She prayed for him. For years she pleaded with him to give up his bad ways. Augustine just laughed.

"I'm having fun, Mother," he said. "Isn't that what counts?"

When Augustine was a young man, he decided to sail to Rome. Monica decided to go along and keep an eye on him. Augustine, of course, did not want his mother to come with him. So when his ship came into port, he made up a lie.

"I've changed my mind," he said. "I'm not going to Rome after all. I'll just go onto this ship for a minute to say good-bye to a friend, and then I'll get off."

"In that case, I'll go to the church to pray," said Monica.

When Monica came out of the church, the ship was gone and her son was gone with it.

Many people would have given up then and there. But not Monica. She followed Augustine to Rome, and when she discovered that he was not there, she tracked him down in the city of Milan.

There she found Augustine up to his old tricks again, going places he should not go and doing things he should not do. Monica refused to give up. She would not let him go. She did not argue with him, though. She lived a quiet, humble life near him, a life full of love for everyone around her, most of all for her son.

Little by little, the mother's patience began to take effect. Augustine began to see that her life was good and full of faith. His proud heart began to melt, and he was ashamed of the way he had acted.

One day Augustine went into a garden alone to struggle with himself about all he had done. He thought about the kind of person he had become, and the ways he had hurt many people around him. He thought about all the years of pain he had brought to his beautiful mother. Bitter tears sprang to his eyes.

Then Augustine heard the voice of a young child playing in a nearby house. He could not tell whether it was a boy or a girl, but the child was singing the words of a song over and over again: "Pick it up and read, pick it up and read."

Augustine raised his head and listened. The words of the song seemed to be calling him: "Pick it up and read, pick it up and read."

He went over to a bench where a copy of the Bible was lying. He picked up the book, opened it, and began to read. Suddenly light flooded into his heart and pushed out all the darkness. He knew that God was calling him to a better life.

He rushed to tell his mother, and when he took her into his arms you can be sure she was the happiest woman in the world. Her son, who had been lost, was found. She knew that all her prayers had been worthwhile. The long years of grief and worry now turned to joy.

Augustine did not disappoint his mother. He served God for the rest of his days and wrote wonderful books that people still read today. He became one of the wisest and holiest men of all time, so wise and holy that today many people call him Saint Augustine.

And as long as he lived, Augustine remembered that he had found his way because his weary mother had kept praying, and drying her eyes, and taking fresh hope for her son.

The Golden Touch

—ADAPTED FROM A RETELLING BY NATHANIEL HAWTHORNE

This Greek myth is a great story for families in our modern age. Sometimes we think we need more golden coins, but often what we really need is more golden times together.

Once upon a time there lived a very rich king named Midas. He had more gold than anyone else in the world, but that was not enough for him. He was happy only when he could get even more gold to add to his treasure. He stored it in great vaults underneath his palace, and he spent many hours a day in his treasure room, counting his coins.

Now, King Midas had a little daughter named Marygold. He loved her very much and said, "She'll be the richest princess in the whole world!"

But little Marygold cared nothing about treasure. She loved her garden, her flowers, and the golden sunshine more than all her father's riches. She was a lonely little girl most of the time, because her father was so busy planning new ways to get more gold and counting what he had that he didn't have much time to tell her stories or go for walks with her.

One day King Midas was down in his treasure room. He had locked the heavy doors and opened his big chests of gold. He piled the gold on the table and handled it as though he loved the touch of it. He let it slip through his fingers, and the clinking was sweet music to his ears.

Suddenly a shadow fell over the heap of gold. Looking up, he saw a stranger dressed in shining white smiling down at him. Midas started up in surprise. Surely he had not failed to lock the door! His treasure was not safe! But the stranger continued to smile.

"You have much gold, King Midas," he said.

"Yes," said the king, "but think how little it is compared to all the gold there is in the world!"

"What! Are you not satisfied?" asked the stranger.

"Satisfied?" said the king. "Of course not. I often lie awake through the long night planning new ways to get more gold. I wish that everything I touched would turn to gold."

"Do you really wish that, King Midas?"

"Of course I wish it. Nothing could make me so happy."

"Then you will have your wish. Tomorrow morning when the first rays of the sun fall through your window, you will have the golden touch."

When he had finished speaking, the stranger vanished. King Midas rubbed his eyes. "I must have dreamed it," he said, "but how happy I would be if it were true!"

The next morning King Midas woke as the sun was rising. He put out his hand and touched the covers of his bed. Nothing happened. "I knew it could not be true," he sighed.

Just at that moment, the first rays of light came streaming through the window. The covers under King Midas's hand became pure gold. "It's true! It's true!" he cried joyfully.

He sprang out of bed and ran around the room, touching everything. His dressing gown, his slippers, and the furniture all became gold. He looked out the window at Marygold's garden.

"I'll give her a nice surprise," he said. He went down into the garden and touched all Marygold's flowers, changing them to gold. *She'll be so pleased,* he thought.

He went back into his room to wait for his breakfast and picked up the book he'd been reading the night before. The minute he touched it, it turned into solid gold. "I can't read it now," he said, "but of course it is far better to have it gold."

Just then a servant came through the door with the king's breakfast. "That looks good," King Midas said. "I'll have that ripe, red peach first."

He took the peach in his hand, but before he could taste it, it became a lump of gold. King Midas put it back on the plate. "It's very beautiful, but I can't eat it!" he said. He took a roll from the plate, but it changed into gold. He took a glass of water in his hand, but that too turned into gold.

"What am I going to do?" he cried. "I'm hungry and thirsty, but I can't eat or drink gold!"

Just then the door opened and little Marygold came in. She was crying, and in her hand was one of her roses.

"What's the matter, little daughter?" said the king.

"Oh, Father! Look what happened to all my roses. They are stiff, cold things!"

"Why, they are golden roses, child. Don't you think they're more beautiful than they were before?"

"No!" she sobbed. "They don't smell sweet now. They won't grow anymore. I like roses that are alive."

"Never mind," said the king. "Eat your breakfast now."

Marygold noticed that her father did not eat, and that he looked very sad. "What is the matter, Father?" she asked, and she ran over to him. She threw her arms around him, and he kissed her. But suddenly he cried out in horror. When he touched her, her lovely face became glittering gold. Her eyes could not see, her lips could not kiss him back, her little arms could not hold him close. She was no longer a loving, laughing little girl. She had changed into a golden statue.

King Midas bowed his head. Great sobs shook him.

"Are you happy, Midas?" he heard a voice say. Looking up, he saw the stranger standing near him.

"Happy! How can you ask that? I am the most miserable man alive!" said the king.

"You have the golden touch," said the stranger. "Is that not enough?"

"Oh, give me back my little Marygold and I'll give up all the gold I have!" said the king. "I've lost everything that was most important."

"You are wiser than you were, King Midas," said the stranger. "Go and plunge in the river that runs at the foot of your garden. Then take some of its water and sprinkle it over anything you want to change back to the way it was before." The stranger vanished.

King Midas sprang up and ran to the river. He plunged in, then dipped a pitcher into the water and hurried back to the palace. He sprinkled the water over Marygold, and the color came back into her cheeks. She opened her blue eyes again.

"Why, Father!" she said. "What happened?"

With a cry of joy, King Midas took his daughter into his arms.

Never again did he care much about gold, except for the gold of the sunshine and the gold of little Marygold's hair.

The Line of Golden Light

—ADAPTED FROM ELIZABETH HARRISON

In this fairy tale, a brave girl's journey to help her sister makes the way easier for other people, too.

Once upon a time there lived a girl whose name was Avilla. She was a sweet, loving child who was always amazed that there were so many things in the world to make her happy.

Now, it happened that Avilla had a younger sister who was blind. She was a beautiful little girl with a heart just as kind and loving as Avilla's, and the two sisters spent most of their time laughing and playing together. More than anything else, Avilla wished her sister could see God's beautiful world, and she kept wondering if there was something she could do to make that happen.

One day Avilla heard of an old, old woman who lived in a dark cave. People said that this old woman knew a secret spell that could give sight to the blind. So one fine spring morning, Avilla went to see her.

The mouth of the cave looked so dark, it made the child's heart beat very fast. But the thought of her little sister gave Avilla courage, and she walked in. She found the old woman sitting on a stone chair, spinning a pile of flax into a fine thread.

Avilla came close to her side and said bravely, "I have come to ask you how I can help my little sister see."

The old woman looked at her for a very long time. Then she stooped and searched in the heap of thread that lay at her side until she found the end of it. She held it out to the child, saying, "Take this and carry it around the world. When you have done that, come to me and I will show you how to give your sister sight."

Thanking the old woman, Avilla seized the tiny thread and hurried out of the cave.

After she had traveled awhile, she looked back to be sure the thread had not broken, since it was so thin. Imagine her surprise when she saw that instead of being a gray thread of spun flax, it was a thread of golden light that glittered and shone in the sun! The tiny line of bright light stretched across the soft green grass, far into the distance. And strange to say, each tiny blade of grass that it had touched had blossomed into a flower. So as the little girl looked back, she saw a flowery path with a glittering line of golden light running through it.

"How beautiful!" she exclaimed. "I did not notice the flowers as I came along, but the magic thread will make the next traveler see them."

Soon she came to a dark forest where sunlight never shone. In the distance she thought she could hear the growl of bears and the roar of lions. Her heart almost stopped beating, but she pushed on. Sometimes she knocked her head against a tree that stood in her way, and sometimes she was afraid she was lost. But every now and then a little gray squirrel would frisk by in a friendly way to let her know she was not alone.

When she looked back, she found that the mysterious thread had opened a shining path behind her, so that the next traveler could easily follow in her footsteps without bumping into trees or stumbling over fallen trunks. That made her happy, and she walked on until she came out of the woods.

But now a new problem faced her. As she trudged along, the air grew hotter and hotter. The trees disappeared, and the grass became brown and dry, until at last she found herself in the middle of a dreary desert. For miles and miles the scorching sand stretched away on every side. Still she toiled on, cheered by a swarm of yellow butterflies that fluttered just ahead of her. Dusty and weary, she finally reached the edge of the desert.

She turned to look once more at the golden thread that trailed behind her, and what did she see? Tall shade trees

had sprung up along the path she had traveled, and each tiny grain of sand that the wonderful thread had touched was now changed into a diamond, a ruby, an emerald, or some other precious stone.

Avilla thought happily of how cool and shady the desert path would be for the next traveler, and of the precious jewels she had left for someone else to gather. She could not stop for them herself. She wanted to press forward and finish her task, so that her little sister might see.

After a while she came to a place where huge rocks lay around in great confusion, as if giants had hurled them at each other. The path grew steeper and steeper and the rocks sharper and sharper, until they cut her feet and tore her dress. A high mountain of rocks lay before her, so tall the child thought she could never get across it. But two strong eagles soared overhead, and their cries seemed to say, "Be brave and strong and you will meet us at the mountaintop!"

So she climbed on and on, always keeping the soaring eagles in sight. When she finally reached the top, she looked back at the thread of golden light, and another marvelous thing had happened. The rugged path of rocks had been changed into broad and beautiful white marble steps! She knew she had made a pathway for others up the difficult mountain, and her heart was happy.

She traveled on and on and at last reached the dark cave of the strange old woman who had told her to carry the line of light around the world. Avilla rushed inside and cried, "I did what you told me to do! I carried the thread all the way around the world! Now please give sight to my sister!"

The old woman sprang to her feet, seized the thread of golden light and exclaimed, "At last! I am free!"

Then, before Avilla's own eyes, the old woman changed into a beautiful young princess with golden hair and kind blue eyes. Her story was soon told. Hundreds of years before, she had been changed into a bent old woman and shut up in the dark cave because she, the daughter of a king, had been selfish and lazy, thinking only of herself. Her punishment had been that she must remain in the cave until she could find someone who would be kindhearted and brave enough to make the long, dangerous journey around the world for the sake of others.

She showed the child Avilla how, by dipping the golden thread into a spring of fresh water, she could change the water into golden water that glittered and sparkled like liquid sunshine. Filling a bowl, they hurried to where the little blind sister sat. The beautiful princess told Avilla to dip her hands into the bowl of enchanted water and then press them upon the closed eyes of her sister. They opened—and suddenly Avilla's little sister could see.

After that, the beautiful young princess came and lived with Avilla and her sister and taught them how to do many wonderful things, but I do not have time to tell you about them today.

Elizabeth's Roses

This legend is about Saint Elizabeth of Hungary, who devoted her life to the poor eight hundred years ago. It reminds us that husbands and wives should respect each other's work.

A long time ago in the kingdom of Hungary, a beautiful daughter was born to the king and queen. All the people loved the little princess, who was named Elizabeth. As a young girl, Elizabeth always had a kind smile and gentle words for anyone she met. And as she grew up, she spent her time trying to make life better for those in need.

When Elizabeth was old enough, she married a nobleman named Louis, and together they lived in a land called Thuringia. Louis was a serious and quiet man who was several years older than his young bride, and sometimes Elizabeth felt a bit in awe of him. Still, they loved each other very much. Before many years had passed, they had four children, and their home was a happy place.

But even after she had a family of her own to care for, Elizabeth never stopped doing everything she could to help those who were suffering in Thuringia. Sometimes she would send a little food to a family she knew was hungry. Sometimes she would visit sick children, sitting beside their beds and telling them stories.

Louis admired his wife's kindness and generosity, but he had his own ideas about the way a princess should act, and he did not like to see Elizabeth always visiting the common people. He did not think it looked right for a noblewoman to stand in the street talking to a peasant, and sometimes he grew angry about her trips to the rougher parts of town.

One winter day when Louis had ridden out to hunt with some of his friends, Elizabeth left the castle and made her

way down the snow-covered path to visit a poor family. She carried several loaves of bread in her cloak, as many as it would hold. The road grew icier as she trudged along, and her load of bread made the walking hard. She did not want to lose her balance, so she was careful to keep her eyes on the path.

Finally, with a sigh of relief, she reached the bottom of the hill. When she looked up, to her dismay, she saw her husband and his friends returning early from the hunt.

Elizabeth stopped in her tracks. She wasn't sure what to do. She would have left the path and ducked into the woods until the hunting party had passed, but there was no time. In a minute the horses were clopping all around her, and the riders were peering down at the young princess standing alone in the snow, holding the bulging folds of her cloak in her arms.

Her husband smiled tenderly when he saw her. Riding to her side, he reached down and placed his hand on her shoulder.

"Where are you going, my dear?" he asked.

Elizabeth did not know what to say. She knew how Louis felt about her habit of walking out alone to visit poor people in wretched huts, and she did not want to anger him in front of all his highborn friends by telling him about her errand. She shrank from her husband and drew her bundle closer to her heart while she searched for the right words.

Louis saw that something was wrong and gazed at her with a clouded brow.

"What are you carrying in your cloak?" he asked. As he spoke, all the courtiers and huntsmen drew closer to see.

Elizabeth looked up at her husband. She knew that all these knights and noblemen might laugh if they saw what she carried, and she thought she might not be able to bear their scorn. Before she really knew what she was saying, she blurted out, "Roses!"

She blushed with shame the minute she spoke. She knew that what she had said was wrong. She would have given anything just then to be brave enough to admit she had lied, but the thought of the hunters' laughter kept her silent. She

could only hang her head and clutch at her cloak with trembling hands.

Looking down at her, Louis guessed the truth. Half of him felt sorry for his struggling wife, but the other half felt angry that she would embarrass him this way in front of his friends. Leaning from his saddle, he reached for her cloak.

"Let me see," he said firmly.

Taking a corner of the cloth, he drew it aside.

And then a marvelous thing happened. In the folds of the cloak he saw not the loaves of bread he had expected. He found roses—glowing red and white roses, as fresh and soft as only flowers can be, even though the season was winter. The sweet scent of summertime filled the air like the richest perfume.

For a moment nobody spoke. Louis looked with wonder into Elizabeth's face for a while. Then he took one crimson rose from the cloak, placed it next to his heart, and bent down to kiss his young wife.

"Go your way, my love," he said gently. He turned his horse and rode with the others back to the castle.

Elizabeth stood in the frozen road for a moment, breathless and astonished. Then she slowly continued down the path, hardly knowing what to think. When she reached the house of the poor family she meant to visit, she opened her cloak, and her eyes grew round with wonder. Once again, her arms were full of the loaves of bread she had carried away from the castle. Only one bright red rose was left in her cloak.

She placed it next to her own heart to remember her love for her husband.

What Does Little Birdie Say?

—Alfred, Lord Tennyson

Our parents watch over us and take care of us until it is time for us to leave home.

What does little birdie say
In her nest at peep of day?
"Let me fly," says little birdie,
"Mother, let me fly away."

Birdie, rest a little longer,
Till the little wings are stronger.
So she rests a little longer,
Then she flies away.

What does little baby say
In her bed at peep of day?
Baby says, like little birdie,
"Let me rise and fly away."

Baby, sleep a little longer,
Till the little limbs are stronger.
If she sleeps a little longer,
Baby too shall fly away.

The Wright Brothers

With dreams and hard work, these two brothers changed the world.

Wilbur Wright was eleven years old and his brother, Orville, was seven when their father came home holding something behind his back.

"Boys, I've got a surprise for you," he said, and he tossed something into the air. When the boys reached to catch it, it rose and flew right over their heads to the other side of the room. It was a toy flying machine made out of paper and wood, with two little propellers spun by a rubber band.

Wilbur and Orville could hardly believe their eyes. They held their breath as the little machine flew overhead. In those days, you see, there were no such things as airplanes and jets and space shuttles. Only birds and bugs and bees knew how to fly. So if you had lived way back then and had seen a little toy fly across a room all by itself, you would have held your breath too.

The two boys called the toy the Bat, and they played with it until it fell apart. Then they built their own small copies and sent them soaring across their yard. They tried to build a much bigger copy too. They wanted to be able to climb inside it and fly above the treetops. The big one never got off the ground, though, so they gave up on the experiment.

When Wilbur and Orville grew up, they opened a bicycle shop in Dayton, Ohio. Bicycles were brand-new inventions and almost everybody wanted one, just as they do today. The Wright brothers were good at fixing and building bikes. They made their own parts in the shop. As they worked side by side, sometimes they would start humming the same tune at the exact same time. When they talked, everyone said they sounded just alike.

They never forgot about the toy flying machine their father had brought home. Sometimes, as they worked, they started thinking the same thing: *I wonder if we could really build a machine that would let people fly*. They watched birds soaring and gliding in the skies above Dayton and kept turning the question over in their minds. *If a bird can fly, why not a man?*

Before long, the Wright brothers were back at work on the problem. This time, they were not going to give up so easily.

They built huge kites called gliders to test the winds. At first the gliders did not work very well. They wouldn't turn the way they were supposed to. They couldn't carry enough weight. Every time Wilbur and Orville got one problem fixed, another one popped up. Their gliders kept slamming into the ground.

Lots of people laughed and said it was silly to try to make a machine that would fly. The Wright brothers didn't listen. Their father had taught them that hard work pays off, and they believed it.

Month after month, folks in Dayton heard hammering, sawing, and filing in the Wright brothers' bicycle workshop. Orville and Wilbur were working away on their flying machine.

One cold, gray December day, the Wright brothers stood among the sandy dunes beside the ocean in North Carolina. They had built their machine, and now they had brought it to a place called Kitty Hawk to see if it would work.

Kitty Hawk was the perfect place to test their *Wright Flyer*. The winds blew almost every day. The sand was soft. And there were no trees or barns or fences to run into.

But that day the wind was blowing almost *too* hard. It howled across dunes and threw sand into the brothers' faces. Low gray clouds moved across the sky. Even the seagulls were staying on land.

Wilbur looked worried.

"This wind is blowing harder than I like, Orv," he said.

Orville grinned.

"This is the day we're going to fly, Will," he said. "This is our day."

The *Wright Flyer* was a funny-looking machine with two big wings made out of cloth, held together with sticks of wood, wires, and string. The people from the village of Kitty Hawk said a man would have to be crazy to climb into a thing like that. It sat on the end of a wooden track, rocking in the wind.

The brothers started the motor. It popped and coughed and roared to life. The propellers spun. Chains rattled. Black smoke poured out of a pipe. The whole machine started to shake. It looked as if it might fall apart.

Orville and Wilbur had flipped a coin to see who would try to fly it. Orville was going to be the pilot. The two brothers stood beside their machine and clasped hands as if it might be the last time they would ever see each other.

Orville climbed aboard and gave the signal. The *Wright Flyer* slowly rolled into the wind.

Wilbur held on to the tip of one wing and walked alongside the machine as it crawled forward. Soon he was running. The *Flyer* was picking up speed. Then Wilbur let go.

It was up—the *Flyer* was up! It rose off the track and flew right into the wind. Orville Wright was flying!

Then, almost before they knew what had happened, it was back on the ground. That first flight was only 120 feet long. You've seen people throw balls farther than that. It lasted only twelve seconds—about as long as it would take you to walk across a room. But it was the first airplane flight in the history of the whole world.

There was one person Orville and Wilbur could not wait to tell about their flight. You can probably guess who it was. That afternoon they walked four miles up the beach to the weather station at Kitty Hawk to send a message to their father: *Success!* They promised to be home by Christmas.

Airplanes today, of course, are much bigger, faster, and more powerful. But every single one of them is descended from that clumsy wood-and-cloth machine Wilbur and Orville flew that long-ago winter.

The next time you see a jet flying way overhead, remember the two brothers named Wright who worked together so that people could take to the air—and the gift from their father that started the whole adventure.

The Hill

—Adapted from Laura Richards

Sisters and brothers help each other along.
They help each other up backyard hills and other climbs in life.

A sister and her little brother stood at the bottom of a hill.

"I can't make it to the top," said the brother. "This hill is too tall. I'll never be able to climb it as long as I live. I'll be stuck here at the bottom for the rest of my life."

His big sister thought about that for a minute.

"That's too bad," she said. "But look—I know a game we can play. Take a step and see if you can make a clear footprint in the dirt. Look at mine! I can see every single line in my footprint. Now you see if you can do it."

The brother took a step.

"Mine is just as clear!" he said.

"Do you think so?" asked his sister. She stepped forward and made another footprint. "See mine? I step harder than you, because I'm older and heavier, so the print is deeper. Try again."

"*Now* mine is just as deep!" cried the brother. "See? Here, and here, and here. Mine are just as deep as yours."

"That's pretty good," said the sister, "but now it's my turn. Let me try again, and we'll see."

They kept going, step by step, matching their footprints and laughing about who could make the clearest, deepest print.

After a while the brother looked up.

"Hey!" he said. "We're at the top of the hill!" He was surprised and very proud.

"Well, what do you know?" said his sister. "We are, aren't we? You made it after all! All you had to do was take one step at a time!"

The sister smiled, and her little brother smiled back. Then they sat down side by side and enjoyed the view from the top of the hill.

Little Eyes upon You

—Edgar Guest

Here are two great poems for big brothers and sisters.

There are little eyes upon you
And they're watching night and day.
There are little ears that quickly
Take in every word you say.
There are little hands all eager
To do anything you do,
And a little boy who's dreaming
Of the day he'll be like you.

You're the little fellow's idol,
You're the wisest of the wise.
In his little mind about you
No suspicions ever rise.
He believes in you devoutly,
Holds that all you say and do
He will say and do, in your way,
When he's grown up just like you.

My Little Sister

I have a little sister,
She's only two years old.
But to us at home that love her,
She's worth her weight in gold.

We often play together,
And I begin to find
That to make my sister happy,
I must be very kind.

And always very gentle
When we run about and play,
And never take her playthings
Or little toys away.

I must not taunt or tease her,
Or very angry be,
With the darling little sister
That God has given me.

The Legend of the Hummingbird

*The way we act at home is very important,
because we will probably act the same way when we grow up and leave home.
This story comes from South America.*

In a land far away lived a mother who had four daughters, named Margarita, Emilia, Carmen, and Maria. The three eldest girls were lazy and rude and rarely obeyed their mother. Only the youngest, Maria, did what she could to be a loving daughter.

The time came when the mother called her children together.

"You are growing older now, and so am I," she told them. "I won't be able to take care of you forever. You must learn to work so you can make your own ways in the world someday. So I have chores for you to do. Margarita, you must dust away the cobwebs. Emilia, you must sweep the floor. Carmen, you must rake the yard. And Maria, you must weed the garden."

Margarita, the eldest daughter, scowled.

"Dust? I can't be expected to dust!" she hooted. "I need my beauty sleep." She packed her bag and left the house to find a quiet place to lay her head.

Emilia, the next daughter, threw up her arms and paced the room in circles.

"I don't know how to sweep," she grunted. "I'm sure I can't learn how. I'm going for a stroll in the countryside. It's much more pleasant there."

She packed her bags and left the house.

Carmen, the next daughter, banged her fist on the table.

"I don't know how to work either!" she shrieked. "I've got better things to do, you know. I'm moving to town. People there know how to have fun."

She too packed her bags and left the house with a frown.

Only Maria, the youngest daughter, put on a smile.

"Don't worry, Mother," she said. "I'll work in the garden and plant as many flowers as it will hold and sell them in town at the market. That way I can stay and take care of you as you grow old."

Time passed, and Maria kept her word. Her garden flourished, and so did her business at the marketplace, and she made enough money to help out her mother.

At last the old woman grew sick and feeble. She sent Maria to find her sisters and bring them home so that she could see them again.

Maria found Margarita asleep in the shady forest.

"Mother is ill and asks you to come home," she told Margarita.

"I'm sleeping right now," Margarita said, yawning. "It's much too early. Tell her I'll come later."

Maria found Emilia wandering in the countryside, searching the fields for scraps of food left from the harvest.

"I don't have time to come home," Emilia said. "I'm hoping to pick up some dinner."

Maria found Carmen walking the town lanes and alleys, knocking on door after door, looking for handouts.

"I can't come home just now," Carmen muttered. "No one feels generous today. I must keep knocking if I am to eat." She turned her back to rap on another door.

Maria returned to her mother, who grew very sad when she heard what her daughters had said.

"My Margarita will live in the dark forest for the rest of her life, sleeping the days away," she cried. "My Emilia will spend her life wandering aimlessly, content to live on what lies on the ground. My Carmen will knock and knock for the rest of her days, grubbing for morsels. Only you, Maria, will be welcomed and loved by all."

And her words came true.

Many years later, Margarita became an owl, and to this day she dwells in the darkest parts of the forest, sleeping the days away.

Emilia turned into an ugly vulture and now circles the country skies, hoping to dine on whatever she finds lying on the ground.

Carmen changed into a woodpecker, and you can still hear her knocking and knocking all day long, grubbing for morsels.

As for little Maria, she is still hard at work in her garden, tending her flowers, sipping nectar from their silky cups. Everywhere she goes, she is welcomed and loved, for Maria turned into a hummingbird.

Teddy Roosevelt: Family Man

The twenty-sixth President of the United States never forgot that his most important job was being a parent.

When Teddy Roosevelt was born, his mother looked at him and said, "He looks like a turtle!" Maybe that's why he always liked the outdoors so much.

As a boy, Teddy spent every spare minute outside, looking at plants and animals. He hunted for beetles, chased dragonflies, and splashed after minnows. He filled his notebook with pictures and writings about everything he saw.

Pretty soon the treasures he found were running and crawling all over the Roosevelt house. His parents found a snake in the water pitcher. They found snapping turtles tied to the laundry tub.

One day Teddy was walking down the road when he met a lady he knew. He tipped his cap to say hello, and a frog jumped out.

Teddy gathered his best finds and opened the Roosevelt Museum of Natural History in his house. He had seashells, birds' nests, a few rocks, a snakeskin, and a seal's skull. At first he kept them in his bedroom, but his mother said all those bugs and nests made it hard to keep the place clean, so he moved his museum to a big bookcase in the upstairs hallway. He charged visitors a penny to see the collection, but he let children in free, as long as they helped feed the live animals.

Teddy loved all kinds of learning, and he spent a lot of time reading and writing. His father taught him to help people in need, tell the truth, and always try to be brave. His mother read him stories about Davy Crockett, Daniel Boone, and the brave cowboys in the West. Teddy wanted to grow up to be just like them.

But even though he was full of energy, Teddy was a sickly child. He suffered from asthma, an illness that made it very hard for him to breathe. Sometimes he could not get enough breath to blow out the candle beside his bed.

Many nights he had to sleep propped up on pillows or sitting in a chair. Only his father could make him feel better. Mr. Roosevelt would gather the little boy in his arms and walk up and down the room until Teddy could sleep. Sometimes he would bundle Teddy up, put him in the carriage, and speed through the cold, dark streets of New York City to help the boy get air in his lungs.

When Teddy was ten years old, his father took him aside. "Son, you have a strong mind," he said, "but you do not have a strong body. You must *make* your body."

Teddy threw back his head. "I will make my body," he promised.

His father bought him a punching bag and some weights, and Teddy set to work building his muscles. Day after day he lifted weights. He pulled himself up on bars and took boxing lessons.

Every summer, his father took him to the country to help him build his strength. Teddy ran barefoot with his sisters and his brother. He picked apples, gathered hickory nuts, and, of course, chased all the frogs he could find. He went hiking in the woods and swimming in the ocean.

Over time, Teddy's muscles did grow strong. He built a powerful body. His chest widened, and he could breathe more easily. He grew up to be a large, sturdy man with a bushy red mustache, a broad smile, and a big, booming voice.

Teddy married a beautiful woman named Edith and had his own family. He had two daughters, named Alice and Ethel, and four sons, named Ted, Kermit, Archie, and Quentin. He called all his children his bunnies.

No one ever packed more into life than Teddy Roosevelt. He did all sorts of grand things. He climbed mountains and wrote books and fought in a war. He roped steers and rode bucking broncos with cowboys. He became governor of New York, and then President of the United States.

But of everything he did, he loved being a father most of all. He thought his own father had been the best father in the whole world, and he wanted to be just like him.

When Teddy became President, he moved his family into the White House in Washington, D.C. The White House is an important place, but the Roosevelt children filled it with laughter. They roller-skated in the hallways. They walked up and down the stairs on stilts and slid down the banister into parties. They hid inside closets and sprang out at visitors when they walked by.

Teddy was very busy as President, but he and his children always made time to be together. They raced on the White House lawn and had pillow fights in the bedrooms. They played soldiers with garbage can lids for shields and wooden sticks for swords. When they played hide-and-seek, the President always insisted on being It.

And of course, they had all kinds of pets. They had a dog named Sailor Boy, a badger named Josiah, a lizard named Bill, a mouse named Nibble, and a parrot named Loretta that could say "Hurrah for Roosevelt!"

Once, when Archie was sick in bed, Quentin decided that a visit from their favorite pony would cheer him up. So he brought the pony into the White House, put him on the elevator, and took him upstairs to Archie's room. And Archie did get better.

Whenever he could, Teddy took his children and their friends into the country, just as his own father had taken him, to hike and fish and swim. Sometimes they would camp overnight and build a big fire, and Teddy would tell scary ghost stories.

Sometimes they would sail from the White House down the river past Mount Vernon, which is where George Washington lived and was buried. When they passed by that spot, Teddy would make the children stand at attention while he rang the ship's bell.

"We're passing the very first President's house and all the things he loved," Teddy would say. "George Washington was the father of our country and a great man, and we should always honor his name."

When Teddy's children grew up and moved away, he wrote them letters telling them how much he loved them and how proud he was to be their father. He wanted them to be fine men and women, so he wrote to them about helping people in need, and telling the truth, and always trying to be brave. All of Teddy Roosevelt's letters have been put into books, and someday, when you are older, you may want to read them for yourself. If you do, you will learn many wise and wonderful things.

The Place of Brotherhood

Brotherhood means giving to each other.
It means helping without being asked, even when no one is looking.

Back in the days of King Solomon, there lived two brothers who were farmers. Their houses were only a short distance apart, and the fields where they grew wheat lay next to each other. These brothers loved each other very much and always looked out for each other.

One night, during the time of year when all the farmers were busy harvesting their crops, the younger brother sat in his house, thinking.

My brother is married with three little children to feed, he mused. *I'm going to share some of my wheat with him.*

Later that night he crept out of his house and into his field, where the bundles of wheat he had cut earlier that day lay stacked on the ground. He took a few bundles, carried them into his brother's field, and piled them onto the stack of wheat there. Then he went home.

A little later that same night, the older brother sat in his own house, thinking.

My brother hasn't married yet, and he's all alone, he thought. *He doesn't have anyone to help him with his harvest. I'll give him some of mine.*

So he got up, went into his own field, and gathered a few bundles of wheat. He carried them into his brother's field and put them on the stack there. Then he went home.

When the sun came up the next morning and the two brothers went into their fields, each was surprised to find that he had just as much wheat as before. Each scratched his head but didn't say anything about it.

That night, they secretly tried to help each other again. As soon as it was dark, the younger brother stole out of his house, gathered a few bundles of his wheat, and put them into his brother's field. A little while later, the older brother left his house and did the same thing.

When the sun rose the next morning, each was astonished to find that he still had the same amount of wheat in his own field.

That night they both decided to try one more time. They slipped out of their houses, picked up as much wheat as they could carry, and started out with their gifts. This time, though, they met right as they got to each other's fields. They dropped the wheat, threw their arms around each other, and thanked God for the blessing of family.

It is said that when King Solomon heard of their love, he built the temple of Israel there at the place of brotherhood.

Jane Addams and Hull House

Here is the story of a woman who showed the world what it means to be a good neighbor.

Jane Addams was six years old when she set out with her father one day on an errand. They passed through a poor part of town, where the streets were shabby and all the houses looked sad.

"Why do people live in such horrid little houses built so close together?" Jane asked.

"They don't want to live here," her father explained, "but these people are very poor. Most of them never went to school. They don't have a chance to move to nicer homes."

Jane thought about that for a minute and made up her mind.

"When I grow up, I'm going to have a great big house," she said. "But it's not going to be on a nice street with other big houses. It's going to be right in the middle of horrid little houses like these. And the children who don't have a chance to play at home can come and play in my yard."

You might not expect a person to stick to a promise like that, especially if she made it when she was only six years old. But Jane's father had taught her that we are put on this earth to help each other, and she never forgot her promise.

When Jane grew up, she went to the great city of Chicago and looked in the poorest part of the town, where the buildings were dirty, the sidewalks were broken, and the cobblestones in the streets were worn away. The air smelled of all the trash lying around. Many of the houses had no running water.

In the middle of this dingy neighborhood, Jane found an old brick mansion with a wide, friendly porch. As soon as she saw it, she knew it would be her home. Many years before, a man named Charles Hull had built it. So the name of the place was Hull House.

Jane began cleaning up the old place and turning it into her home. She scrubbed the floors and hung pictures on the walls. Her friends were horrified. They warned her not to move into such a dirty, run-down neighborhood. But Jane knew it was a place where she could do much good, and it wasn't long before some of her friends came to join her.

The people of the neighborhood did not know what to make of these clean, well-dressed young ladies who had moved into Hull House. What did they want? Why in the world had they come there, when they could live someplace much nicer?

At first the neighbors kept their distance, but soon they noticed the warm smiles of the ladies sitting on the big, friendly porch. They began coming up the steps to say hello. Before long, Jane and the ladies of Hull House were making friends.

Every day, as she sat on her porch, Jane saw little girls and boys running in the crowded streets. Their mothers and fathers worked all day long, and the children had no place to go. Jane knew they needed a good friend, so she told their parents she would look after them. Before long, Hull House was full of the sounds of babies laughing and children playing in the halls.

Jane knew that boys and girls like to be outdoors, and it made her sad to think that the only place these children had was the streets. So she got a man who owned some old buildings to knock them down and build a playground in their place. She had promised her father many years before that children would come and play in her yard, and now her promise was coming true.

One evening Jane and her friends gave a party for their neighbors at Hull House, and they had candy for all the children. But when the candy dish came around to one group of girls, they sadly shook their heads and said, "No, thank you." They worked all day long in a candy factory, they said, and could not stand the sight of anything sweet.

In those days, you see, children of poor families often worked in hot, dusty factories from seven o'clock in the morning until nine at night. It broke Jane's heart to think of boys and girls bending over loud, noisy machines. So she went straight to the governor and helped make a law to keep little children out of the factories.

That was Jane's way. Whenever she saw a neighbor in need, she tried to help. The doors of Hull House were never locked. It was a place for people to come together and share a meal, listen to music, and swap stories. Jane and her friends started a library so that poor families could have books to read. They held art classes for children and their parents. They visited the sick and helped people find jobs.

Even when she grew old, Jane still lived at Hull House. Anyone who came to her doorstep could always find welcoming arms. Until the day she died, Jane was a good friend to the people who needed her most. All her neighbors loved her, and she became one of the most admired people in the whole country.

Jane Addams had made a promise to her father, and she kept it. She turned a great big house into a home that made the world a better place to live.

The Baby

—George MacDonald

Here is a great poem to read when a new baby sister or brother arrives.

Where did you come from, baby dear?
Out of the everywhere into the here.

Where did you get your eyes so blue?
Out of the sky as I came through.

What makes the light in them sparkle and spin?
Some of the starry spikes left in.

Where did you get that little tear?
I found it waiting when I got here.

What makes your forehead so smooth and high?
A soft hand stroked it as I went by.

What makes your cheek like a warm white rose?
Something better than anyone knows.

Whence the three-cornered smile of bliss?
Three angels gave me at once a kiss.

Where did you get that pearly ear?
God spoke, and it came out to hear.

Where did you get those arms and hands?
Love made itself into hooks and bands.

Feet, whence did you come, you darling things?
From the same box as the cherub's wings.

How did they all just come to be you?
God thought about me, and so I grew.

But how did you come to us, you dear?
God thought of you, and so I am here.

Louisa May Alcott's Dream

Louisa May Alcott's love of family led her to write one of the world's best-loved books for young people.

A thick New England snow flew around Louisa May Alcott's home in Concord, Massachusetts. Outside, snowbanks covered fences and bushes. Inside, Louisa sat with her three sisters in front of a cheerful fire, laughing and telling stories.

Suddenly they heard a loud knock. A neighbor stood at their door.

"I'm sorry to trouble you," the man said, "but our baby is sick, and our house is cold. We've run out of wood to burn. May we have some of yours?"

Louisa watched her mother and father closely.

"I don't know," Mrs. Alcott said slowly. "We don't have much wood ourselves. What if we run out? Where will we get more?"

Mr. Alcott smiled. "Let's give them half our wood and trust in the Lord," he said.

Louisa's mother thought it over.

"Well, I guess they need it more than we do," she said. "If our wood gives out, we can always get into bed and tell stories."

Without any more talk, they gave away half of their firewood.

As evening fell, the winds blew harder, the snow fell more thickly, and cold drafts crept into the Alcott house. Louisa shivered and wondered if their fire would last the night.

Then came another knock, and a second neighbor stood at their door.

"Good evening, folks," he said. "Do you need any wood? I've got some extra pieces in my shed, and you're welcome to them."

Soon the Alcotts' fire was blazing again. Its warmth and cheer filled the room.

"Never be afraid to give to others," Louisa's father said. "It always comes back to you, one way or another."

Louisa looked at her mother and father. She loved them so much, she thought she might burst. They were always taking care of other people.

Someday, when I'm older, I'm going to take care of them! Louisa promised herself.

Louisa knew that her family was poor. Her father was a schoolteacher. All his students loved him, but he never seemed to make much money. Sometimes the Alcotts had nothing to eat but bread, fruit, and milk. Louisa swapped old clothes with her sisters instead of buying new ones. They did not have many pretty things, and there were few presents when Christmas came each year.

Still, even though they were poor, the Alcotts were a happy family. Mr. Alcott taught his daughters the alphabet by twisting his body into the shapes of the letters, which made the girls laugh. Mrs. Alcott read them stories like "Cinderella" and "Jack and the Beanstalk," which made their eyes grow round with wonder.

Most of all, Louisa loved spending time with her sisters, Anna, Elizabeth, and May. No matter how hard the times, they found plenty of fun. Sometimes they roamed the woods around their house picking berries, trotting like horses, or pretending to be fairies. Sometimes they stitched old rags into costumes and staged their own plays in the attic. In the evenings, they sang and laughed around the piano. They were happy as long as they were all together.

When Louisa wanted to be alone with her thoughts, she would slip away and sit with her back against an old cartwheel that lay half buried in the ground near the house. There she dreamed of becoming a writer.

Someday I'll write wonderful stories that everyone will want to read, she told herself. *I'll be famous and earn enough money to make life easy for Mother and Father.*

Louisa practiced writing stories whenever she could. She wrote tales about flowers and elves that she read aloud to her sisters. She wrote poems and letters to her parents. Her father taught her to write in a diary. One year her mother gave her a pencil case for her birthday because she knew Louisa loved to write.

"You'll grow up to be a great writer, you'll see!" Mrs. Alcott said.

Time passed, and Louisa became a young woman. She managed to make a little money for her family by sewing and teaching in a school of her own. But she never gave up her dream of writing.

One day she gathered her courage and took one of her stories to a man named Mr. Fields who ran a famous magazine in Boston. *Maybe he'll like it and print it,* she told herself.

She sat nervously in Mr. Fields's office amid piles of books and papers while he read her precious story. When he was finished, he looked up.

"Stick to your teaching, Miss Alcott," he said. "You can't write."

Louisa walked out of the office with tears in her eyes.

I don't believe him! she told herself. *I'll show him. I* will *be a writer.*

Louisa refused to give up. She wrote and wrote, and before long she was earning money here and there by selling her stories to magazines. Then one day she decided to write a book for girls.

She sat down to think. Who were the girls she knew best? Her sisters, of course. And what were the happiest times she knew? The times she spent with her family. If she could write about those, maybe she could write something wonderful.

Louisa began to dream of the people she would put into her book. Her own sisters, Anna, Elizabeth, and May, became sisters named Meg, Beth, and Amy. Louisa turned herself into a girl named Jo.

Her pen began to move over her paper, and suddenly the four sisters were alive and talking.

"Christmas won't be Christmas without any presents," grumbled Jo, lying on the rug.

"It's so dreadful to be poor!" sighed Meg, looking down at her old dress.

"I don't think it's fair for some girls to have plenty of pretty things, and other girls nothing at all," added little Amy, with an injured sniff.

"We've got Father and Mother and each other," said Beth contentedly, from her corner. . . .

Stories kept flowing from Louisa's pen, stories she invented from her memories about growing up. She wrote about playing games, picking berries in the woods, making up plays, and all the other things she and her sisters had done. Louisa wrote down everything she loved about her family. When she was done, she held a book in her hands. She called it *Little Women.*

Then something marvelous happened. A publisher agreed to print *Little Women,* and when it went on sale in the bookstores, people rushed to buy it. Everyone wanted to read about the joys and troubles of the four sisters named Meg, Jo, Beth, and Amy.

And so Louisa's dream came true. She became a writer after all. Her books made her wealthy and famous. She could take care of her family and make sure they were never in need again, just as she had promised herself she would.

Best of all, many years later, young people everywhere still love *Little Women*. Louisa May Alcott's famous book still brings smiles to readers' faces and joy to families all over the world.

A Father's Return

This wonderful tale from Africa reminds us just how much family members need each other. Children need their parents, and parents need their children.

There once was a man who thought of himself as the happiest man alive because he had a loving wife and four healthy sons. The oldest son was named Keen-Eyes because he could follow tracks through field and jungle better than anyone else in the village. The second son was known as Sharp-Ears because he knew the call of every creature in the wilderness. The third son was named Strong-Arms because he could win any contest of strength. The fourth son was only a baby, but his father was sure the boy would grow up to be as skilled and devoted as his brothers.

One morning the family woke to discover that the father had disappeared. By nightfall he had not returned, and the next morning brought no sign of his whereabouts.

They talked it over and wondered where he might have gone.

"Maybe he decided to visit our uncle," said Keen-Eyes.

"Or maybe he went to the festival in the next village," suggested Sharp-Ears.

"Or he may have gone into the hills to enjoy the cool mountain breezes," said Strong-Arms.

Their mother remained quiet and shook her head. She was worried.

Another day passed, then another. Still their father did not return. Keen-Eyes, Sharp-Ears, and Strong-Arms were not sure what to do. They waited and wondered.

One morning, as the baby sat on his mother's lap, he opened his mouth and spoke his first words:

"Where is Father? I want my father."

His older brothers gazed at him. Suddenly, they knew they had to do something.

"That's right," said Keen-Eyes. "Where is Father?"

"Some harm may have come to him," said Sharp-Ears.

"We have to look for him," said Strong-Arms.

The three older brothers started out at once, following a path deep into the jungle.

"Look, he came this way," said Keen-Eyes, pointing. "I can see his tracks on the trail." He led his brothers across hills and valleys, through fields and woods, farther and farther from home. But finally the tracks disappeared, and even Keen-Eyes lost the trail.

"We have to give up," he said.

"Wait!" said Sharp-Ears. "I hear someone crying out."

He led his brothers even deeper into the wilderness, farther than they had ever gone before, pausing every now and then to strain for the sound only he could hear.

At last they came to a rushing river. Beside it lay their father, holding a growling leopard at bay with his spear.

"We must save him!" yelled Strong-Arms, and without waiting for his brothers, he threw himself onto the crouching beast and crushed it in his mighty grasp.

"You came just in time," gasped their father. "I went into the jungle to hunt, but I fell from a tree and hurt my leg. I could not make it home. I've lived on what food I could find, but my strength was failing and the leopard moved in for the kill."

His sons wrapped his wounded leg. They brought food to build his strength and carried him home to their village. Everyone listened to the story of how Keen-Eyes, Sharp-Ears, and Strong-Arms had saved their father. Everyone praised their skill and devotion.

But all the talk went to the brothers' heads, and they began to argue about who had done the most to rescue their father.

"If not for me, we would never have known which way to look," said Keen-Eyes. "I followed his trail deep into the jungle."

"Yes, but you lost it," said Sharp-Ears. "I heard him cry out, and I found him beside the river."

"What good would that have done if I had not been there?" asked Strong-Arms. "I was the one who killed the leopard and saved our father from certain death."

They argued with each other and finally asked their father to decide who had done the most to save him.

He raised his hand for quiet.

"I owe my life to all three of you," he told them. "You each played a part in my rescue. But if you ask which of my sons did the most to bring me home, I must tell you that it is not you, Sharp-Eyes, or you, Keen-Ears, or even you, Strong-Arms. The one who truly brought me home is here."

He took his youngest son in his arms.

Then everyone remembered that this was the son whose first words had been "Where is Father?" Those words had stirred his older brothers to action. The little boy's loving and aching heart had brought their father home.

Hush, Little Baby

One of the most beautiful sounds in any home is the sound of a lullaby.

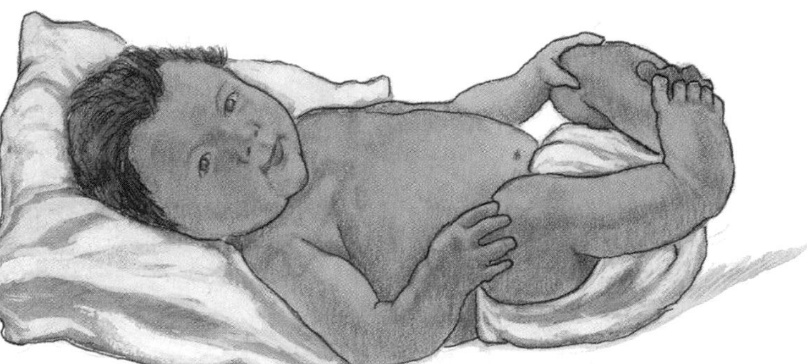

Hush, little baby, don't say a word,
Papa's going to buy you a mockingbird.

And if that mockingbird won't sing,
Papa's going to buy you a diamond ring.

If that diamond ring turns brass,
Papa's going to buy you a looking glass.

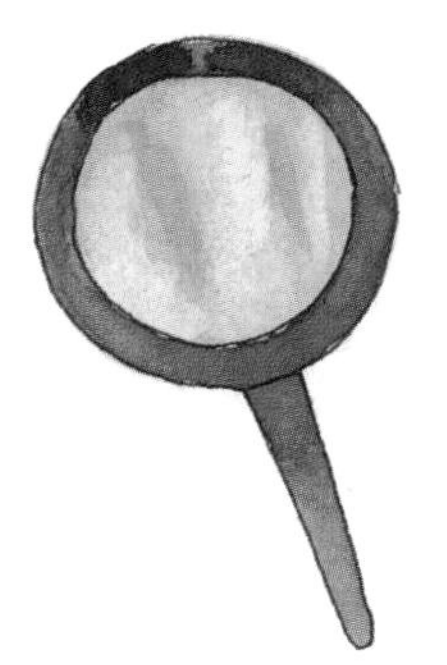

If that looking glass gets broke,
Papa's going to buy you a billy goat.

If that billy goat won't pull,
Papa's going to buy you a cart and bull.

If that cart and bull turns over,
Papa's going to buy you a dog named Rover.

If that dog named Rover won't bark,
Papa's going to buy you a horse and cart.

If that horse and cart fall down,
You'll still be the sweetest little baby in town!

The Husband Who Was to Mind the House

Here's a story about a fellow who learns that work done around the home is just as hard and just as important as any other job.

Once upon a time there was a man who was so grumpy and cross, he never thought his wife did anything right around the house. One evening, during the time of year for cutting hay, he came home complaining that dinner wasn't on the table and the cow had not been put into the barn.

"I work and I work all day," he growled, "and you get to stay at home. I wish I had it that easy. I could get dinner ready on time, I'll tell you that."

"Dear love, don't be so angry," said his wife. "Tomorrow, let's switch places. I'll go out in the fields and cut hay, and you stay here and do the work at home."

That sounded good to the husband. "I could use a day off," he said. "I'll do all your chores in an hour or two and sleep the afternoon away."

So early the next morning, the wife put a scythe over her shoulder and trudged out to the hayfield to mow hay. The husband stayed behind to do all the work at home.

"First I'll wash a few clothes," he said to himself, and he filled the tub and washed away. Next he decided to churn some butter, so he went to the kitchen and filled the churn with cream. He churned and churned and churned some more, for they must have butter at dinner. Then he remembered that he needed to hang the clothes up to dry. He went into the yard and had just finished hanging his shirts on the line when he saw the pig run into the kitchen.

"Uh-oh," he said to himself. "That rascal might do some damage." He dashed into the kitchen, but as soon as he got through the door, he saw that the pig had knocked over the churn. It was having a merry old time oinking and rooting around in the cream, which was running all over the floor.

"You no-good beast!" the man shouted, and ran after the pig. He caught it, but it was so slippery from the cream that it shot out of his arms and right back out the door.

The man raced into the yard, bound to catch that pig no matter what, but he stopped dead in his tracks when he saw his goat. It was standing beside the clothesline, chomping away on his very best shirt.

"Get away from there, you scoundrel!" the man yelled. He tied up the goat, ran off the pig, and took what was left of his shirt from the line.

Then he went to the dairy and found enough cream to fill the churn again. He churned and churned and churned some more, for they must have butter at dinner. Suddenly he remembered that their cow had been in the barn all night and had not had a mouthful to eat or drink all morning, though the sun was high.

"I'd better take her out," he told himself. He thought the meadow was too far to take her, so he decided to put her on top of the house, for the roof, you see, was thatched with grass. The house stood next to a steep hill, and he thought that if he laid a wide board from the side of the hill to the roof, he could easily get the cow onto the housetop.

He didn't want to leave the churn, though. He was afraid the pig might come back. "I've learned my lesson," he told himself. "I won't let that rascal knock it over again."

So he put the churn on his back and went out with it. On the way to the barn, he decided he'd better give the cow some water before he put her on the roof, so he got a bucket. As he bent over the well to draw the water, the cream ran out of the churn, over his shoulders, down his back, and into the well.

"Blast it!" he yelped. "It's almost dinnertime, and I still don't have any butter yet. I'd better hurry."

He went to the barn, got the cow, and led her up the hill behind the house. He found a nice wide board and laid it between the hillside and the roof. Then he carefully led the cow across. He left her on the rooftop, happily munching the grass.

"Now to the butter," he told himself. He dragged the churn back into the kitchen and filled it with more cream. Just then an unhappy thought struck him: *That stupid cow might fall off the roof and break her neck.*

"I know how to fix that," he said. He climbed back onto the roof to tie her up. He fastened one end of a rope around the cow's neck, and he slipped the other end down the chimney. Then he went back inside and tied the rope around his own waist.

Now at last he could churn the butter. He churned and churned and churned some more, for they must have butter at dinner. But while he was hard at it, down fell the cow off the housetop after all, and as she fell she dragged the poor man up the chimney by the rope. There he stuck, halfway up. As for the cow, she hung halfway down the wall of the house, swinging between heaven and earth.

Meanwhile the wife, who was out in the field, waited and waited for her husband to call her to dinner. Finally she thought she'd waited long enough and went home.

When she got there and saw the cow hanging halfway down the wall of the house, she ran up and cut the rope with her scythe. As soon as she did, down came her husband out of the chimney. When she went into the kitchen, she found him standing on his head in a porridge pot.

“Welcome back,” he said after she had fished him out. “I have something to say to you.”

He said he was sorry, gave her a kiss, and never complained again.

The Bundle of Sticks

—AESOP

Brothers, sisters, mothers, and fathers can give each other strength.

A man had seven children who were always getting angry and arguing with each other. The older they got, the less time they wanted to spend together. They hardly spoke to each other at all, unless it was to fight.

One day their father called them all together and showed them seven sticks tied in a bundle.

"I want each of you to try breaking this across your knee," he said. The children passed the bundle around. One after another, they tried breaking it, but it was too thick and strong.

Then the father untied the bundle and handed each of the seven children a stick. "Now," he said, "see if you can break that over your knee."

Now that they had only one stick apiece, the children could easily break them.

"There, you see?" said the father. "Alone, you're much weaker. If you quarrel and drift apart and can't depend on each other, you'll have a hard time in life. When problems come, they may break you.

"But if you stick together, love each other, and each take your share of the load, our family will be strong," he said. "When bad times come, we can make it through them together."

Penelope's Web

—Adapted from a retelling
by James Baldwin

Here is one of the greatest homecoming stories ever told.

Of all the heroes who fought against Troy, the wisest and shrewdest was Odysseus, king of the island country called Ithaca. Odysseus did not want to go to war. He wanted to stay home with his wife, Penelope, and their baby boy, Telemachus. But the princes of Greece demanded that he help them.

"Go, Odysseus," said Penelope. "I will keep our son and the kingdom safe until you return."

So Odysseus sailed away to the Trojan War. The whole time he was gone, he thought of little else except returning to Ithaca. He longed for the sight of his wife and son.

Twenty long years passed. Telemachus grew up to be a tall, strong young man. The war ended, and the other Greek heroes returned to their homes. But there was no sign of Odysseus.

"His ships must be wrecked, and he must be dead, lying at the bottom of the sea," the people said.

Penelope alone still hoped. "Odysseus is not dead," she insisted. Every day his seat was placed at the table for him, and his great bow, which hung in the hall, was polished.

"How foolish of her," the Greek chiefs and princes said. "Everyone knows that Odysseus is gone for good. She should marry one of us now."

Soon the chiefs and princes began sailing to Ithaca, hoping to win Penelope's love. They were vain, foolish fellows. "We have come as suitors for your hand," they told Penelope. "Odysseus is never coming home. Choose one of us."

"Give me a while longer to wait for him," Penelope pleaded. She pointed to a loom that held a half-finished cloth. Its pattern was so rich and full of color, it looked like a beautiful spider's web gleaming in the morning sun. "If Odysseus fails to return by the time I've finished weaving this cloth, I will choose one of you," she said.

The suitors agreed and made themselves at home in the palace. They took the best of everything. They feasted every day in the great hall and helped themselves to the wine in the cellar. They were rude and insulting to the people of Ithaca.

Every day, Penelope sat at her loom and wove. "See how much I've added to the cloth?" she would say. But at night, when the suitors were asleep, she took out all the threads she had woven during the day. That way she was always at work, and the cloth was never finished.

As the weeks passed, the suitors grew tired of waiting. One night, instead of going to sleep, one of them crept through the palace and peeped into the weaving room.

There he saw Penelope busy unraveling the cloth by the light of a little lamp.

The next morning, all the unwelcome guests knew the secret. "Fair queen," they said, "you are very cunning, but we know what you are doing. Tomorrow you must choose one of us. We will wait no longer."

The next day the suitors gathered in the great hall. They ate and drank and shouted so much that the timbers of the palace shook.

While they were feasting, Telemachus came in and began to take down all the shields and swords that hung on the walls.

"What are you doing with those weapons?" shouted the suitors.

"They are dull with smoke and dust," said Telemachus. "They will keep much better in the treasure room. But I will leave my father's great bow, which hangs at the head of the hall. My mother polishes it every day and would miss it if it were gone."

"She won't be polishing it much longer," the suitors laughed. "Before this day is over, Ithaca will have a new king."

At that moment a ragged, barefoot beggar entered the hall.

"What do you want here, Old Rags?" yelled the suitors. "Get out!" They hurled crusts of bread at his head. They stopped when they saw Penelope coming down the stairs, stately and beautiful, with her servants around her.

"The queen! The queen!" cried the suitors. She has come to choose one of us!"

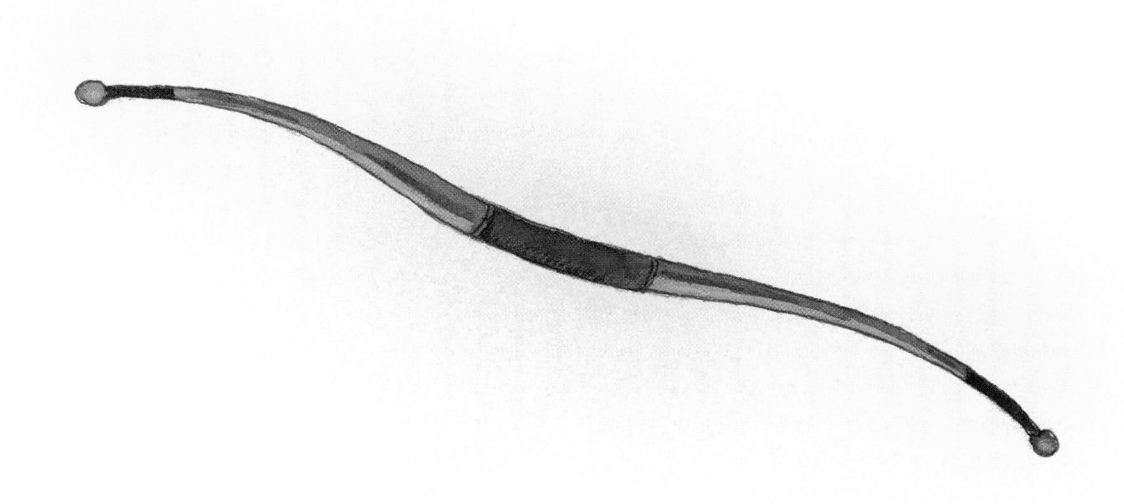

"Telemachus, my son," said Penelope, "what poor man is this?"

"Mother, he is a wandering beggar who washed up on our shores last night," answered the prince.

"Then he must have something to eat," said Penelope, "and when he has eaten, he can tell us his story."

But the suitors, who had gathered around the feast table, started shouting again. "This beggar can tell us his tale tomorrow! It's time for you to choose a new husband! Choose now!"

"Chiefs and princes," Penelope said in a shaking voice, "let us leave this decision to the gods. Behold, there hangs the great bow of Odysseus. He was the only one who was able to string it. Let each of you try his strength in bending it. I will choose the one who can shoot an arrow from it most skillfully."

"Well said!" cried all the suitors, and they lined up to try their strength. The first took the huge bow in his hands, struggled to bend it, then threw it on the ground. "Only a giant could string a bow like that," he said.

One by one the suitors tried to string the bow, but all failed.

"Maybe the old beggar would like to join this contest," they said, sneering.

The ragged beggar rose from his seat and went with halting steps to the head of the hall. "Methinks," he said, "that in my younger days I once saw a bow like this."

"Enough! Enough!" shouted the suitors. "Get out, you old fool!"

Suddenly a great change came over the stranger. Almost without effort, he bent the great bow and strung it. Then he rose to his full height, and even in his beggar's rags he looked every inch a king.

"Odysseus!" Penelope cried.

The suitors were speechless. They looked for weapons, but Telemachus had taken all the shields and swords off the walls. In wildest alarm, they turned and tried to escape from the hall. But the arrows of Odysseus were swift and sure, and not one missed its mark. "Now I avenge myself upon those who have tried to destroy my home!" Odysseus cried. One after the other, the lawless suitors perished.

The next day Odysseus sat beside Penelope and told her of his long wanderings over the sea. He told her how he had washed up on the shores of his own island, made himself known to Telemachus, and asked him to remove the weapons that hung in the great hall.

Penelope, in turn, told how she had faithfully kept the kingdom all those long years, as she had promised, even when the wicked suitors came. Then she brought from her chamber a roll of soft, gleaming fabric. "This is the cloth, Odysseus," she said. "I promised that on the day I finished it, I would choose a husband. It is done now, and I choose you."

Odysseus was home at last.

The Bridge Builder

—Will Allen Dromgoole

This poem helps us remember the things our grandparents have done for us.

An old man, going a lone highway,
Came at the evening, cold and gray,
To a chasm, vast, and deep, and wide,
Through which was flowing a sullen tide.
The old man crossed in the twilight dim.
The sullen stream had no fears for him.
But he turned, when safe on the other side,
And built a bridge to span the tide.

"Old man," said a fellow pilgrim, near,
"You are wasting strength with building here.
Your journey will end with the ending day.
You never again must pass this way.
You have crossed the chasm, deep and wide—
Why build you the bridge at the eventide?"

The builder lifted his old gray head.
"Good friend, in the path I have come," he said,
"There followeth after me today
A youth, whose feet must pass this way.
This chasm, that has been naught to me,
To that fair-haired youth may a pitfall be.
He, too, must cross in the twilight dim.
Good friend, I am building the bridge for *him*."

Grandmother's Table

—Adapted from the Brothers Grimm

Having grandparents or great-grandparents nearby is a special gift. Treat them with love and respect.

Once there was a feeble old woman whose husband died and left her all alone, so she went to live with her son and his wife and their own little daughter.

Every day the old woman's sight dimmed and her hearing grew worse. Sometimes at dinner, her hands shook so much that the peas rolled off her spoon and the soup splashed out of her cup. The son and his wife frowned at the way she spilled her meal all over the table and onto the carpet. One day, after she had knocked over a glass of milk, they told each other that enough was enough.

They set up a small table for her in the kitchen, in a corner next to the broom closet, and made the old woman eat her meals there. She sat all alone with tear-filled eyes. Sometimes the son or his wife would stand nearby and talk to her while she ate, but usually it was to scold her for dropping a bowl or a fork.

One evening just before dinner, the little granddaughter was busy playing on the floor with her blocks, and her father asked her what she was making.

"I'm using my blocks to build a table," she said. "I'll put it in the corner for you and Mother so you can eat by yourselves when I get big."

Her parents thought about what she had said for a minute, and suddenly they both began to cry. That night they led the old woman back to her place at the big table. From then on, she ate with the rest of the family, and her son and his wife didn't seem to mind a bit if she spilled something every now and then.

All the World Is Sleeping

Our parents are always thinking about us, even through the night.

Go to sleep upon my breast,
All the world is sleeping.
Till the morning's light you'll rest,
Mother watch is keeping.

Birds and beasts have closed their eyes,
All the world is sleeping.
In the morn the sun will rise,
Mother watch is keeping.